RED STAR RISING

RED STAR RISING

SOVIET FIGHTERS

DOUG RICHARDSON

HAMLYN

First published in 1989 by
The Hamlyn Publishing Group,
a division of The Octopus Publishing Group Ltd
Michelin House, 81 Fulham Road, London SW3 6RB

© The Hamlyn Publishing Group 1989

Colour artworks: © Pilot Press, Octopus Books Ltd

Series Editor: Len Cacutt

Designer: Brian Folkard

Production: Hilary Stephens

Typeset by MS Filmsetting Limited, Frome, Somerset

Printed and bound in Spain by Gráficas Estella, S.A. Navarra.

ISBN 0600 564 371

Contents

Chalk v. Cheese

If the day ever comes when Warsaw Pact and NATO air-crew can meet in large numbers at international air shows, mix freely, buy each other beers and talk flying the initial discussions will probably hinge around 'What's your aircraft like to fly'. Given sufficient time, the pilots of East and West would then turn to more mundane matters such as as 'How did you see our air power in earlier years – what to your side seemed our greatest strength?'

WarPac pilots would probably speak of the West's 'hot' fighters such as the F-15, F-16, and Mirage 2000, and the nuclear threat posed by advanced strike aircraft such as the F-15E and Tornado. Their NATO counterparts would in turn draw the image of facing massive numbers of aircraft turned out by production lines apparently blessed with an inexhaustible supply of money, metal and orders.

At a first glance, it would be easy to make the mistake of thinking that the huge force of fighters and attack aircraft based in Eastern Europe is simply a mirror image of that deployed by NATO. This is not the case.

NATO sees its advantages as lying in areas such as aircraft quality and performance, the skills of its pilots, and the flexibility of its tactics. On the other side, different standards apply. Quantity and reliability are thought to count more than all-out quality, while cen-

tralization and standardization are seen as virtues.

With the exception of small numbers of Orao 'Jurom' strike aircraft based in Romania, far from the main front line in central Europe, all the aircraft operated by the Warsaw Pact allies are of Soviet design and manufacture. Most of the NATO allies have their own work-hungry aircraft industries, a problem not faced by Bulgaria or East Germany. Those Eastern allies who do have a national industry built little in the way of military aircraft. Czechoslovakia, Romania and Poland build piston and jet trainers, while Romania also builds the Orao in conjunction with Yugoslavia, and that's it.

The aircraft with which the Soviet Union equips its own air force and those of its allies tend to be simpler than those in NATO service, but combat experience has often shown that the performance is there where it counts. It is easy to smile at equipment which needs a major overhaul every few hundred hours, but even easier to miss the point that between those overhauls the aircraft, radar or missile may require much less maintenance than its NATO counterpart.

Right: The Sukhoi Su-24 is the Soviet Air Force's most potent tactical strike aircraft. This Fencer C was photographed over the Baltic in 1984 by the Swedish Air Force.

MiG or Mirage?

Several years ago, I had the chance to talk to an experienced test pilot who had flown Eastern and Western aircraft, indcluding the MiG-21, Mirage III, and another Western Mach 2 fighter of the 1960s and early 1970s. I asked how they compared?

He started by dismissing the third, unnamed plane, as indeed did most nations which bought that generation of Mach 2 aircraft. His verdict that it was a pedestrian and uninspired design was reflected in the type's poor sales record. Choosing between the MiG and Mirage was more difficult. For peacetime, he backed the Mirage, saying that the French aircraft was more comfortable to fly, and had a much better cockpit layout than the MiG, a factor he predicted would result in fewer mistakes by the pilot, and thus fewer crashes. If asked to go to war, however, he would back the MiG, explaining that its high maneuverability would give a well-trained pilot the edge in combat.

An American writer once described the early model MiG-21 as looking as if it had been built by half-trained assemblers. He was probably right, to judge by contemporary photos, but my test pilot acquaintance was prepared to trust his life to the Soviet fighter should its country go to war.

An Aviation Classic

The MiG-21, assigned the ugly reporting name 'Fishbed' by NATO, is an aviation classic. It first flew more than 30 years ago, entered service in 1958, and was to remain in production until 1987. It has probably the long-

The MiG-21 offers acceptably high performance and a more than acceptable price, so it has proved a popular export fighter. This is a MiG-21FL of the Indian Air Force, a version based on the Soviet MiG-21PF, and built under licence by Hindustan Aeronautics.

Right: MiG-21PF Fishbed D of the Egyptian Air Force, an early version now largely phased out.

Right: For several years following the 1967 Six Day War, the MiG-21PF played a major role in Egypt's air defense, despite that country's insistance that a better aircraft was needed to match Israel's new F-4 Phantoms.

Right: Following the loss of several Soviet-flown MiG-21s in air combat near the Suez canal, the Soviet Union finally agreed to supply Egypt with the MiG-21PFMA Fishbed J.

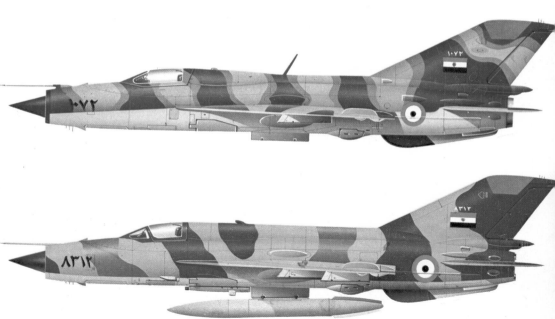

est production run of any jet fighter; the equivalent of the Sopwith Camel staying in production until well into World War II, or the P-51 Mustang rolling off the line until the outbreak of the Vietnam War.

In the Soviet Union, the aircraft has already been superseded by the later MiG-23, but it is still the most common aircraft in service with the Warsaw Pact. With the exception of Bulgaria, all the East European allies field at least 100 MiG-21s, and some have more than 300.

Nation	Fighter	Recce	Trainer
Bulgaria	80 PFM		
Czecho-slovakia	280 F/PF/ PFM/MF	40 RF	30 U/US/ UM
East Germany	200 FL/PFM/ MF	12 RF	20 U/UM
Hungary	100 F/PF/PFM		
Poland	350 PF/FM/ PFM	35 RF	25 U
Romania	150 F/PF		15 U
Soviet Union	720 PF/PFM/ MF/bis	60 RF	

Like the Supermarine Spitfire of World War II fame, the MiG-21 spawned a near-endless series of variants. The key to understanding these is to realise that there were only four main production types which can be categorised by their design bureau 'Ye' series designation. Most production variants belong to one of these basic types.

The Ye-6 was a basic day fighter, and carried a simple ranging radar within its intake centrebody. The initial version was known to NATO as Fishbed A, and was quickly followed into service in 1959 by the MiG-21F Fishbed C, the first version to enter full production. By modern standards, this was a modest aircraft, weighing only 18,000 lb (8,200 kg) at the most, and with only 12,675 lb (5,750 kg) of installed thrust. It was powered by the Tumanski R-11F-300 tubojet, an uprated version of the 11,240 lb (5,100 kg) thrust R-11 used in the earlier Fishbed A. The latter had been armed only by a pair of NR-30 30 mm cannon, but the MiG-21F lost one of its guns to make way for the avionics needed to handle the AA-2 Atoll heat-seeking missile. The aircraft normally carried two of these Sidewinder look-alikes, and measured target range using the simple High Fix radar. A two-seat MiG-21U trainer version was also produced. Czechoslovakia, Hungary and Romania still operate the MiG-21F, which must be regarded as obsolete.

As the West proved to its own satisfaction, the usefulness of such simple fighters was found to be limited. Pilots needed an effective radar set able to locate targets. To meet this need, Mikoyan created the Ye-7 series of radar-guided interceptors. By eliminating the taper applied to the forward fuselage of the Ye-6, his engineers were able to make room for a larger radome housing an R1L Sapphire radar (known to NATO as Spin Scan).

Right: Two SU-7 Czechoslovakian scramble from a hard strip. These planes have seen long service with all the Warsaw Pact signitories. Unusually for the front line Czech Air Force, these aircraft are not seen with camouflage.

Right: The MiG-21MF was the most widely-produced version of the series. It introduced the uprated R13-300 engine, Jay Bird radar, and a much-needed air-data system. Despite these changes, it retained the NATO designation Fishbed J used for the earlier MiG-21PFMA.

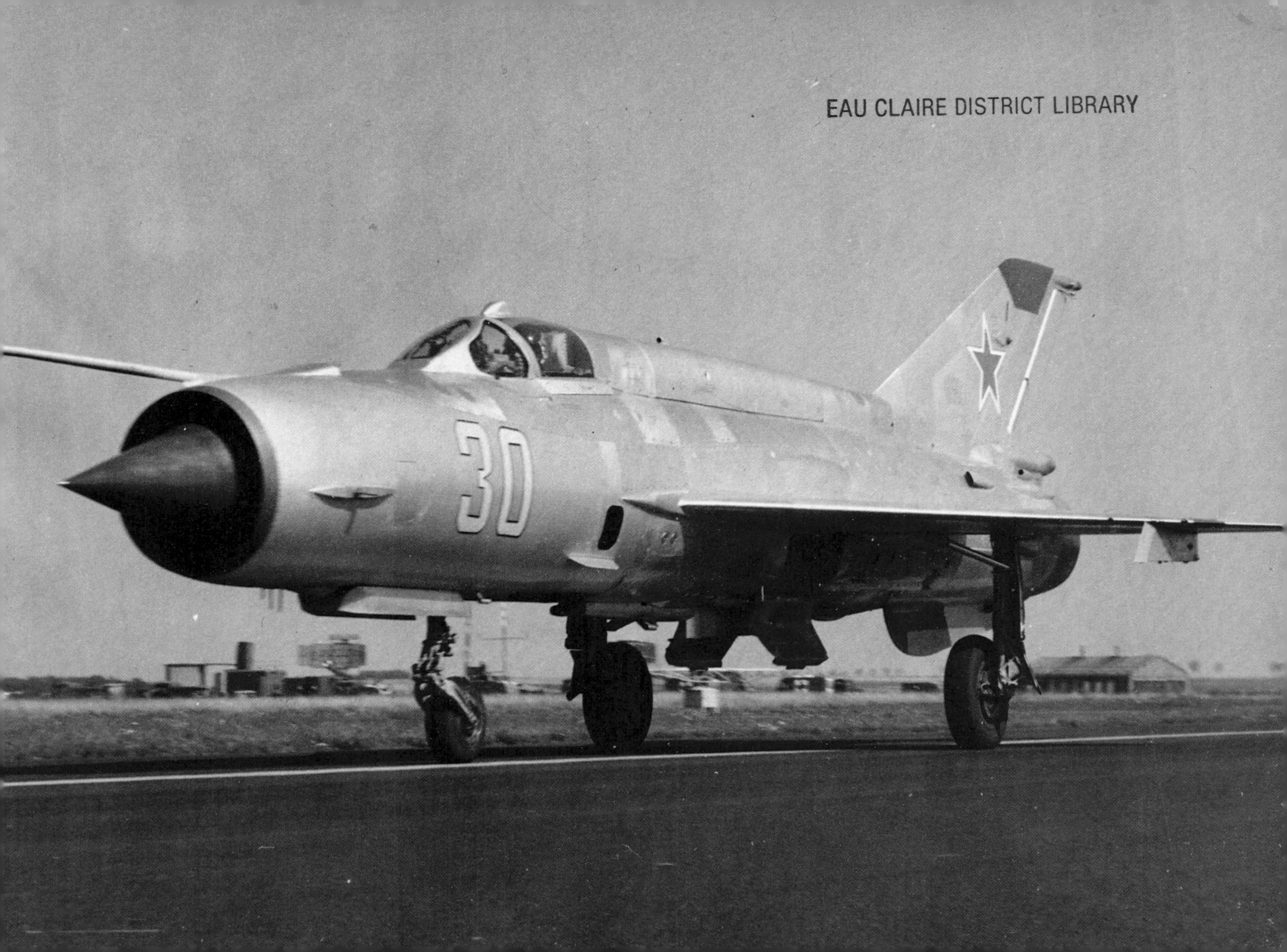
30

Take-off weight inevitably increased, so a 13,100 lb (5,950 kg) thrust R-11F2S-300 engine was installed, along with larger fuel tanks. The single 30 mm internal cannon carried by the Ye-6 was removed, the canopy design was revised, and a dorsal spine was added to the fuselage. This missile-armed fighter was designated MiG-21PF, and built in two versions known to NATO as Fishbed D and E. The D model had a narrow Ye-6-style tail fin, while the E introduced a redesigned fin of wider chord. MiG-21PFs still serve with Czechoslovakia, Hungary and Poland.

Another move which offset the increased operating weight was the use of blown rather than slotted flaps. First aircraft so fitted were known as the Mig-21PF(SPS) and -21PFS. This was followed by the MiG-21FL. Developed for India, this was a broad-tailed PF fitted with the uprated R-11F2S-300 engine and an R2L export radar. The Indian Air Force had also insisted that a gun be fitted. There was no

Right: During the 1971 Indo/Pakistan War, Indian Air Force MiG-21FL fighters were operated in a hastily-applied camouflage finish.

Right: Indian-built MiG-21FLs also formed the equipment of that nation's Red Archer aerobatics team.

room in the fuselage for a gun, so the neat GP-9 gun pack was devised for ventral mounting. This contained an unusual weapon, the twin-barrel GSh-23 cannon.

The Ye-7 family was completed by the MiG-21PFM Fishbed F. This was powered by the R-11-F2S-300 engine, and had the SPS flap-blowing system, plus a new sideways-hinging canopy and a KM-1 zero-zero ejection seat. Two trainer versions of the Ye-7 were also developed. The MiG-21US used the R-11F2S-

300 engine, while the later MiG-21UM had the R-13.

At this point, the Mikoyan team created the Ye-9 family by redesigning the airframe to suit the MiG-21 to multi-role combat operations, toughening the structure, adding two more wing pylons plus provision for a belly-mounted GSh-23 gun pack, and fitting a larger dorsal fairing. They probably intended to fit Tumanski's new R-13 engine, but this may have hit development problems. The first Ye-9

Left: MiG-21MF of the East German Air Force. This side view shows how the size of the dorsal spine first used on the M-21PF was increased in depth on these third-generation MiG-21s.

Left: This Soviet Air Force MiG-21PF interceptor is a relatively early example, retaining the narrow-chord vertical tail used on previous models.

Yugoslav Air Force 8 Sqn,

Indian Air Force

Iraqi Air Force

variant was the R-11F-powered MiG-21PFMA Fishbed J, which soon gave way to the MiG-21MF. This introduced the new R-13-300 engine, the much-improved Jay Bird radar, and an air-data system.

Eroding the MiG 21's Performance

Despite the increases in engine power, this process of gradual evolution may have eroded the MiG-21's performance. In 1975, the British aviation magazine 'Flight International' interviewed a Third-World pilot who had trained in the Soviet Union on the MiG-21MF. He drew a jaundiced view of the aircraft, claiming that for practical purposes, maximum top speed was only Mach 1.9, while the useful combat ceiling was only around 46,000 ft (14,000 m). General performance was 'extremely poor above 20,000 ft', while a problem with the aircraft's center of gravity made the final 800 litres of the aircraft's 2,600-l internal fuel capacity was virtually unusable. Burning it would move the c/g out of limits, a situation which could result in the aircraft pitching nose-up at low speeds when the pilot attempted to land. (The test pilot of my acquaintance (see p. 8) had flown the much earlier MiG-21F, and denied that any pitch-up problem existed on that model.)

Although a simple export reconnaissance version had been designed around the MiG-21F, development of a practical model suitable for Warsaw Pact service had to await the birth of the Ye-9 series. Warsaw Pact MiG-21R reconnaissance aircraft are based on the 21PFMA, and carried its camera or electronicsintelligence (elint) payload in a center-line pod. A second version exported to Egypt has no pod, three cameras being mounted under the cockpit floor of the -21PFMA airframe. The later MiG-21RF is an MF fitted with the uprated R-13 engine and a centerline sensor pod. No trainer version of the Ye-9 was developed. The MiG-21UM seems to have been good enough for the task of training pilots assigned to late-model Fishbeds.

Next MiG-21 fighter variant was a curious design destined to serve only with the Soviet Air Force. Only built in modest numbers by MiG-21 standards, the MiG-21SMT Fishbed K carried extra fuel in an even-larger hump-backed dorsal spine, and could carry four AAMs including the new radar-guided AA-A-2 Advanced Atoll. Design objective in this aircraft seems to have been the creation of a longer-ranged model able to serve with the Soviet Air Force until the newer and heavier MiG-23 was available in quantity.

For the fourth and final generation of MiG-21s, the Mikoyan bureau created new versions able to serve as agile multi-role fighters. The massive hump-backed dorsal spine of the MiG-21SMK was abandoned in favour of a slimmer configuration broadly similar to that of the MF. Yet another airframe redesign saw the basic structure further strengthened, with space

Left: Czechoslovak Air Force MiG-21R reconnaisance aircraft with centreline sensor pod.

Left: MiG-21MF assigned to a Soviet Air Force fighter regiment in the Kiev Military District.

being found for additional fuel. In addition to the AA-2, the MiG-21bis could also carry the new AA-8 Aphid IR-guided dogfight missile.

The Tumanski team did its part by providing the new R-25 turbojet, a higher thrust engine similar in dimensions to the R-13 it replaced. The resulting family of aircraft is known as the MiG-21bis, and probably had a new 'Ye' series number. Externally similar to the MiG-21MF it was produced in two forms – the basic MiG-21bis Fishbed L, and the final production model, the broadly similar MiG-21bis Fishbed

N (recognisable by tiny nose- and tail-mounted antennae for the Swift Rods ILS system).

Soviet engine development is always a bit of a mystery, and it is not clear just how much afterburning thrust the R-25 develops. Many sources quote a figure of 16,535 lb (7,500 kg), but some observers report 17,600 lb (8,000 kg) or even 19,800 lb (9,000 kg). Those neat round figures in kilograms suggest that guess-work is being used all round. In the real world, engine thrusts rarely work out in neat, round pound *and* kilogram figures!

MiG OR MIRAGE

This Su-7BM Fitter of 222 Sqn, "The Killers", Indian Air Force, is finished in a three-tone camouflage scheme, but the general effect is rather blunted by the ruddy vertical fin.

VG Surprises for the West

At the July 1967 Domodedovo Air Show, the Soviet Union surprised the West by showing not one but two new variable-geometry (VG) aircraft. One was clearly an adaption of the existing Su-7 Fitter fighter-bomber, and was dismissed by observers as a mere research testbed, but the other was an all-new design by the Mikoyan design team. One look made it obvious that this was an all-new combat aircraft, and a possible match for the best the West could field.

In creating the new VG fighter, Mikoyan bureau engineers drew many of their ideas from contemporary Western technology. Western aircraft design had revealed the desirability of lateral intakes which would leave the nose free for avionics, so the Mikoyan team selected a configuration similar to that used on the F-4 Phantom. The US warplane had been committed to the Vietnam War in the summer of 1965, so it is probable that the Mikoyan team had the chance to examine the structure of examples shot down in action.

The lateral system would feed air to the aircraft's powerplant, a single large turbojet. The only existing engine in the appropriate thrust class was the Lyulka AL-7F, and this was used to power the prototypes, while the Tumanski engine bureau tackled the job of creating a newer and more efficient design, coming up

with the R-27 turbojet, a 22,485 lb (10,200 kg) thrust engine which may have much of its technology in common with the smaller R-25 used in the final versions of the MiG-21.

Although an experimental jet-lift prototype was also built (the Mikoyan 'Faithless'), the Ye-231 was based on a VG wing. Since they were starting from a clean sheet of paper, and thus free of the need to minimize structural changes which had hampered the Su-17 designers, the Mikoyan team was able to locate the critical wing pivots in an F-111 style glove. A single vertical tail surface would not give sufficient stability, so a ventral fin was added. To provide ground clearance, this was arranged to fold sideways.

Flogger Preferred to Faithless

The Ye-231 flew for the first time in the winter of 1966/67. Flight tests soon showed its superiority over the 'Faithless' so the VG design was selected for further development. To help with the development of such a complex aircraft, a small pre-series production run created enough AL-7F-powered aircraft to equip a Soviet Air Force regiment in 1971. Two variants seem to have been built – the basic MiG-23S closely based on the Ye-231, and the MiG-23SM with four pylons located under the wing glove and the inlets. All were known to NATO

Right: Soviet Air Force Su-7B
Fitter A assigned to Frontal
Aviation in the late 1970s.

Right: Two-seat trainer versions
of the Su-7 were developed, but
as this Egyptian Su-7U
(codenamed Moujik by NATO)
shows, the view from the rear
cockpit was minimal.

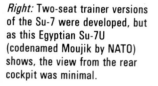

Right: An Su-7 in Algerian
markings.

More than 1,000 Su-7s were built, and the type was the Warsaw Pact's main fighter-bomber in the 1960s and early 1970s. This Czech Su-7 has now been replaced by the newer Su-20/22 variable-geometry version.

Right: The Su-7BM introduced the uprated AL-7-21 engine. This example served with the Czech Air Force.

Right: Final model of single-seat fixed-wing Su-7 series was the Su-7BMK. Similar to the BM, it had better avionics plus two more stores pylons, and was widely exported to Middle Eastern air forces. The aircraft shown here is Egyptian, and has now been retired.

as the 'Flogger A', the reporting name assigned to the Ye-231.

By 1972, the Tumanski R-27 turbojet was available, allowing full production of the MiG-23 to begin. Much to NATO's surprise, the MiG-23MF Flogger B fielded in 1975 turned out to be a rather different aircraft to the pre-series aircraft seen earlier. The exact nature and reason for these changes are a matter of some

controversy. Immediately obvious was the revised outer wing, the chord being increased by moving the leading edge forward. This could not be done on the inboard section due to the glove, so was only applied to the outboard section. This created the effect of a large dog-tooth when the wing was swept, but with the wing in the unswept position produced a narrow slot. The outboard leading-edge exten-

sions also made a convenient stowage for a leading edge slat which occupies the outer two-thirds of their length.

On the revised aircraft, the gap between the trailing edge of the fully swept wing and the leading edge of the tailplane was wider than on the Flogger A, while the jetpipe terminated at the base of the fin rather than extending about 3.5 ft (1.0 m) aft as before. Most observers claim that these differences are the result of the rear fuselage being shortened to match the new engine, while to compensate the effect which this would have on the balance of the aircraft (particularly since the R-27 was lighter than the Al-7 it replaced), the wing pivots and outer wings were moved forward by about 2 ft (0.6 m), shortening the gloves and increasing the gap.

Neither claim is correct, aviation writer Bill Sweetman claimed in 1985. He suggested that the increased gap between wings and tail surfaces was created by moving the latter (and the fin) backwards along the fuselage. The point at which the dorsal extension at the root of the fin blended with the fuselage was left unchanged. As a result, the extension was elongated. Since only a handful of Flogger A photos are available, it is impossible to be dogmatic, but I favour Sweetman's conclusions.

Like Sweetman, I do not believe that the modifications were related to the change in powerplant. Switching engines does not need such drastic modifications, as General Dynamics demonstrated in the late 1970s by re-engining the F-16 with the longer and heavier J79. No design team will embark on a major modification scheme without good reason. Had the changes observed in the Flogger B been intended from the start, they would have been

Above: The MiG-23ML Flogger G has a revised tail fin, new avionics and more effective missiles. This Soviet Air Force example carries AA-7 Apex missiles on the wing gloves and AA-8 dogfight missiles under the fuselage.

present in Flogger A. A more likely reason for the redesign was to eliminate performance shortcomings.

Given the Soviet penchant for large production runs, there are obvious advantages in taking time to get the design right. As a result, the Soviet Air Force has never been over-reluctant to delay production and to redesign the aircraft in the light of flight trials experience. Almost certainly, this is what happened to the MiG-23.

Writing about the MiG-23 in the early 1980s, I suggested that the modifications had been due to stability problems. Given that the Flogger A VG configuration works satisfactorily on the Su-24 Fencer, this now seems unlikely. The changes were probably intended to increase maneuverability, either because flight trials had shown the aircraft to be lacking in this respect, or because revised operational requirements were demanding greater agility.

Flogger B was committed to production on a

Right: This Soviet Air Force MiG-23 combines a number of puzzling features. Its nose radar is the small Jay Bird normally carried by Flogger E export aircraft, but the latter do not have the small sensor fairing seen under the nose section of this Soviet aircraft.

Right: MiG-23MF Flogger B in standard Soviet Air Force air-superiority grey finish. A launcher for unguided rockets seems an unlikely armament for a fighter tasked with air-to-air combat.

Like Most Soviet fighters, the MiG-23 is available in two-seat training versions. This is an Indian Air Force MiG-23U. The rectangular object mounted above the canopy is a mirror — part of a periscope used to give the instructor in the back seat a degree of forward visibility.

Mikoyan MiG-23MF Flogger B

Role: single-seat fighter
Length: 59 ft 5.5 in (14.5 m)
Wingspan: 26 ft 9 in to 46 ft 9 in (8.17–14.25 m)
Weights: empty 24,000 lb (11,00 kg); loaded 35,000 lb (16,00 kg); max. takeoff 42,000 lb (19,000 kg)
Powerplant(s): one Tumanski R-29B turbojet
Rating: 17,600 lb (8,000 kg) dry thrust, 27,500 lb (12,500 kg) with after burner
Tactical radius: 485–700 nm (900–1,300 km)
Max. speed: Mach 2.35
Ceiling: 61,000 ft (18.600 m)
Armament: one 23 mm GSh-23 cannon plus four AA-8 Aphid and two AA-7 Apex missile

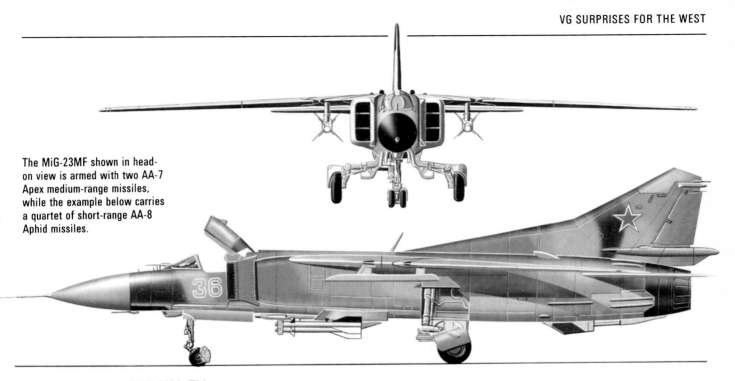

The MiG-23MF shown in head-on view is armed with two AA-7 Apex medium-range missiles, while the example below carries a quartet of short-range AA-8 Aphid missiles.

large scale as the MiG-23M. This was a very different aircraft to the older MiG-21 in engineering and production terms. Its construction required new alloys able to withstand higher stresses. Lighter than earlier materials, they were also of higher purity. The Tumanski engine made similar demands in metallurgy to the airframe in terms of material quality and reliability.

New Aircraft, New Radar, New Weapons

A new aircraft demanded new radar and weapons. To help the MiG-23 find its target, the Soviet electronics industry developed the High Lark radar, a new set broadly in the same performance class as the radar in the F-4 Phantom. For missile armament, Flogger would carry the new AA-7 Apex and AA-8

Right: MiG-23MF in the markings of the East German Air Force. Like the Soviet MF shown on page 24, this aircraft carries a pod for unguided rockets, suggesting that the East Germans see the type as a multi-role fighter.

Above: Flogger E is an export model fitted with simplified avionics and armament. It carries the Jay Bird radar used on late model MiG-21s. This example is Libyan.

Aphid. AA-7 was a semi-active radar missile similar in concept to the US AIM-7 Sparrow, while the tiny AA-8 was an IR-guided dogfight missile better suited to air combat than the older AA-2. Five hard points are provided for ordnance. One is located under each wing glove, one on each side of the lower fuselage, and one on the centerline.

After only a few years of production, the R-27 engine was supplanted by the more powerful R-29B, and the aircraft was redesignated MiG-23MF. This model probably introduced the IR sensor seen under nose of Flogger Bs built after 1977. It was about this time that the aircraft was generally released to the Warsaw Pact. On Soviet Air Force MiG-23s, the R-29 has now

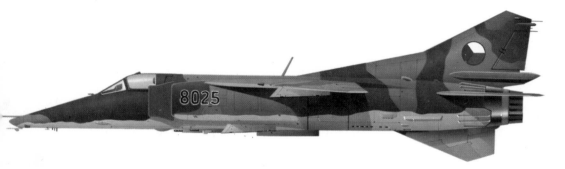

Above: This MiG-23ML Flogger G was one of a Kubinka-based Soviet Air Force unit which visited Finland and France in 1978.

Centre: The MiG-23BN Flogger H (seen here in Czech markings) is based on the earlier MiG-23BN Flogger F export fighter, but can be distinguished by the presence of small fairings on the side of the forward fuselage.

given way to an improved model designated R-29PN, but no details of this engine are available.

Development of a two-seat trainer was only to be expected, and this emerged as the MiG-23U Flogger C. This retained the older R-27 engine, but replaced the High Lark radar with the simpler and lower-performance Jay Bird

set used in late-model MiG-21s. This radar was also used in the MiG-23Ms Flogger E, a single-seat model developed for export. This downgraded aircraft, which never entered Soviet or Warsaw Pact service, also lacks the IR sensor and Doppler radar navaid fitted to Flogger B.

With these basic models in production, along with a dedicated ground-attack version

described later, the Mikoyan bureau embarked on a series of modifications intended to keep the MiG-23 fighter effective through the 1980s and beyond. This was done by improving the avionics and by making aerodynamic changes.

When the resulting MiG-23ML Flogger G (originally reported as the MiG-23bis) was sighted in 1978, the most obvious recognition point was the revised vertical tail fin, which was much smaller than that of the earlier models. This would reduce weight and drag, with the aircraft relying to a greater degree on artificial stability. Avionics changes are thought to include a new and lighter nose radar. Flogger G now serves with the Soviet Air Force, and with the air arms of Czechoslovakia and East Germany.

The next stage involved cropping the size of the ventral strake. To compensate for the lost area, small slots were opened between the glove and the fuselage. Vortices created by these improve flow-back over the glove, improving yaw stability at high angles of attack. Soviet designation of this version is unknown, but NATO has assigned it the reporting name Flogger G. This model, armed with the new AA-11 Archer missile, also has a new IFF system whose antenna may be seen just forward of the cockpit canopy.

Opposite: This view of a Soviet Air Force MiG-23MF Flogger B shows the aircraft's rugged undercarriage, an essential feature on an aircraft intended to operate from front-line airstrips. The small light-coloured fairing on the wing leading edge just above the pylon covers an EW antenna.

The Duck-billed Flogger

In parallel with the deployment and development of the Flogger B, the Mikoyan team also created two specialized ground attack versions. First to be seen was an aircraft which combined a new forward fuselage of duck-bill profile with the standard MiG-23 center and rear fuselage, but it soon became apparent that an all-new design with the same front fuselage was also in service. Deployed in 1975, this was a redesign sufficient to warrant the designation MiG-27. NATO called it the Flogger D.

The duck-billed front fuselage lost its nose radome, and had been redesigned to a configuration reminiscent of the Sepecat Jaguar. A tiny chin-mounted optical post for a laser rangefinder and marked-target seeker make the resemblance even more close. To improve forward visibility, the canopy has been bulged upwards to allow the pilot to be seated higher in the cockpit, while the steeply sloping nose is less of an obstruction to his sightline. Armor was fitted on either side of the pilot, giving the front fuselage a slab-sided look.

At first, the duck-billed MiG-23 was seen as an interim step along the route to the MiG-27 Flogger D. Some probably flew during development of the latter aircraft, but it eventually became apparent that it was a separate subtype in its own right, the MiG-23BN Flogger F.

Changes incorporated in the MiG-27 Flogger D are all intended to match the aircraft to the low-level strike role, and to operations

Right: This MiG-27 Flogger D of the Syrian Air Force shows the general configuration of this ground-attack variant of the MiG-23 design. Note the revised nose (with no radar), simplified air intakes, and the shortened jetpipe.

from rough strips. Descriptions of the MiG-23 undercarriage have included 'an object lesson in robust yet simple design' or – less kindly – as looking as if it had escaped from a World War II Bailey bridge. For the MiG-27, an aircraft due to operate from rough airstrips, it was fitted with improved brakes, larger-diameter nose-wheels, and wider main-gear wheels with low-pressure tires. Stowing the enlarged center main wheels within the already crowded center fuselage involved bulging the lower lines of both the fuselage and the undercarriage doors. The additional diameter of the nose-wheels also resulted in small bulges on their doors. A less-obvious change is the deletion of the inboard tab on the horizontal stabilisers.

Photos of MiG-27s on final approach give the distinct impression that the undercarriage of the strike aircraft extends lower than that of the fighter. Bill Sweetman believes that the MiG-27 undercarriage has modified main beams which give increased ground clear-ance for under-fuselage stores.

The hard points fitted to the fuselage sides on fighter variants were moved to underneath the inlet ducts, thus increasing ground clearance, while two more were provided on either side of the rear fuselage. A single hard point is located under each of the movable outer wing sections, but this is non-swivelling, so can only be used at minimum sweep. These are used for external tanks which can be jettisoned when empty, allowing full wing sweep to be used.

The strike role needed a better gun than the short-barrelled GSh-23 used on the fighter versions of the MiG-23. It was replaced by an externally mounted six-barrelled rotary can-non. Also of 23 mm calibre, this can probably fire 60–80 round per second, but its longer barrels will give greater accuracy than those of the GSh-23. It has been suggested that the gun in trainable in elevation, a feature which would allow it to be kept accurately aligned with its target during low-level attacks.

Operating at low level, the MiG-27 would never attain the Mach 2.0+ top speed of the MiG-23, so the variable inlets used on the latter aircraft could be replaced by a simpler fixed design, while the afterburner is of a revised

Above: **This Royal Norwegian Air Force photograph gave the West its first good view of the Sukhoi Su-27 Flanker fighter and its armament of AA-10 Alamo and AA-11 Archer missiles.**

and slightly shorter pattern. The outer walls of these new inlets were bulged outwards to meet the airflow requirements of the new powerplant. This was the Tumanski R-29-300. Its designation clearly implies that it is a derivative of the basic R-29, and most published accounts suggest that it has a slightly lower thrust of around 17,920 lb (8,130 kg) dry, rising to 25,350 lb (25.500 kg) in afterburner. It is curious, however, that such a downrated engine should require larger inlets. Although it is tempting to speculate that the -300 engine might be a low bypass-ratio turbofan derivative of the R-29, one would have expected to see a new engine designation, also deeper rear fuselage and a larger diameter jetpipe.

Avionics Probabilities

Several small radomes and fairings associated with new items of avionics have also been added. Each wing glove has a small pod built into its leading edge. These fall into three groups: the starboard glove pod has a tiny radome at its front end, and is probably a command link antenna for the AS-7 Kerry command-guided ASM; the port-side pod has a small window, and is probably an electro-optical tracker used with SACLOS (semi-automatic command to line-of-sight) missiles. Two smaller radomes are built into the front end of fairings located on the lower fuselage just forward of the nosewheel doors. These could be antennae for a simple radar-homing

system used to guide the aircraft towards hostile radars.

All MiG-23BN Flogger strike aircraft seem to have the glove radome, but the twin fairings on the lower fuselage sides are present only on the Flogger H version of the -23BN, an aircraft whose export has been restricted to the Warsaw Pact and India. The author has never seen the glove-mounted EO pod on any MiG-23BN.

A second version of the MiG-27 has now been fielded. This is known to NATO as Flogger J. The most obvious recognition points are leading-edge root extensions running from the front edge of the glove to a point just aft of the inlet. The duck nose has been redesigned to incorporate new sensors and a small under-nose blister fairing, while the bullet fairings on the wing gloves have been deleted. Tabs have been added to the horizontal stabilizer, restoring these surfaces to the configuration used on the MiG-23, while the cockpit armor seems to have been removed.

Nation	MiG-23	MiG-23 BN	MiG-27
Bulgaria	—	40	—
Czechoslovakia	50	30	—
East Germany	80	30	—
Hungary	50	—	—
Poland	50	80	—
Romania	—	50?	—
Soviet Union	2,000?	600+	830

Most Western observers dismissed the S-221 VG prototype seen at Domodedovo at the same time as the Ye-231 as a research aircraft, an ugly but low cost adaptation of an existing airframe in order to obtain VG experience. That indeed had been its original purpose when it first flew in August 1966, but flight testing soon showed that this relatively crude adaptation had cured many of the deficiencies of the aircraft on which it was based.

This was the veteran SU-7 Fitter, a swept-wing fighter which had been in service since 1959. Despite the well-documented inadequacies of this big Sukhoi aircraft, the author has always had a soft spot for the Fitter. First flown as the S-1 in 1955, and deployed four years later as the Su-7, it was easy to fly and provided a good and stable weapon platform in the low-level strike role. On the engineering side, its solid construction made it easy to maintain and rugged enough to withstand the stresses to low-level flight.

Following the successful trials of the VG S-22I, work immediately started on a definitive

As the crew of this Indian Air Force MiG-23U trainer demonstrate, keeping the canopy open is an essential aid to crew comfort when taxiing under the hot Indian sun. The second cockpit takes the space used by fuel or avionics in the single-seater. Use of the small Jay Bird radar has created space in the nose for displaced 'black boxes'.

S-32 version. This added a dorsal spine to the fuselage, and was powered by an uprated AL-21F-3 engine offering 24,700 lb (11,200 kg) of thrust. Two additional pylons were mounted on the fixed inner section of the wing, and two more were added under the fuselage, giving the aircraft the ability to carry heavier ordnance loads plus the obligatory external tanks. Fuel capacity had been increased, but by a mere three per cent.

This ground-attack fighter appeared in the early 1970s as the Su-17, and was known to NATO as the Fitter C, and exported to Poland and other customers as the Su-20, a designation which reflected minor internal changes. The Su-17/20 proved an interim type. First deployed in 1976 the Su-17M Fitter D had an extended nose, whose 10 in (25 cm) stretch allowed a more modern nav/attack system to be carried. A shallow fairing under the nose housed a simple-terrain-following radar, and a Doppler navigation radar. This version also formed the basis of the two-seat Su-17UM Fitter E trainer, but on these aircraft the avionics fairing was deleted, and the front fuselage slightly drooped, while the dorsal spine was increased in size as it ran forward, gradually changing into a fairing aft of the rear cockpit, and probably containing fuel.

Power Plants and Logistics

In creating the Fitter F export version of the Fitter D, the Sukhoi team took the unusual step

of changing from the Lyulka AL-21 engine to the Tumanski R-29B used in the MiG-23. Since this boosted the installed thrust by less than three per cent, and required a redesign of the rear fuselage to a slightly bulged configuration, it is obvious that this change was not carried out for performance reasons. The purposes of the change was to simplify logistical support for export customers, many of whom would also operate the MiG-23. The Soviet Air Force, which already had extensive support facilities for the Lyulka engine, found it advantageous to retain this powerplant, and never adopted the Tumanski-powered version of the aircraft. From now onwards, the aircraft would be developed in Su-17 and Su-22 forms.

Fitter F is generally similar to the D but has a small dorsal extension to the fin. In addition to having the R-29B engine, also carries export-standard avionics. It was designated Su-22. Trainer version is the Fitter G, basically an E model with the new engine and a taller tail fin. An equivalent Lyulka-engined model appeared in the Su-17 series, where it serves as a trainer for the new single-seat Su-17 Fitter H. This strike model retains the dorsal fairing aft of the cockpit, but houses its avionics within the fuselage rather than in a chin fairing. It can carry a pair of AS-7 Kerry ASMs. Export equivalent of the H model is the Fitter J, which some users operate as a multi-role aircraft for attack or air-defense. First seen in 1984, the latest Fitter K model is an Su-17 which incorporates a cooling intake extending forward of the fin.

Nation	Su-17	Su-20/22
Bulgaria		
Czechoslovakia		100
East Germany		30
Hungary		40
Poland		90
Romania		
Soviet Union	1,020	

Libyan Air Force Su-22
Fitter F fighters are often
seen carrying AA-2 Atoll heat-
seeking air-to-air missiles. This
aircraft is cruising at subsonic
speed with wing sweep set to
an intermediate angle.

The wing pivots on the
Su-17 (and the Su-20 and -22
export models) are located
about one-third span, creating a
large fixed wing centre section.

Mach 3 Threat to the West

Opposite: The massive power of two afterburning Tumanski turbojets can drive the MiG-25M Foxbat E at speeds of up to Mach 2.8. The aircraft is never seen without pylons, leading some observers to speculate that these supplement the twin vertical tail surfaces.

In 1967 the Soviet Union presented one of history's more spectacular air shows. Held at Domodedovo, this included the public debut of more than half a dozen new types of fighter. Some were experimental prototypes, but three were to be fielded in large numbers. Western observers were surprised by the sight not only of the aircraft which would become the MiG-23, but also by an aircraft for which the commentator claimed a top speed in the Mach 3 class. The idea that the Red Air Force might be about to deploy a new fighter faster than anything which the West possessed other than a small number of SR-71 reconnaissance aircraft was disturbing news to the USAF, which promptly started planning for an aircraft in the same performance class.

Foxbat was developed in response to a 1958 Soviet Air Force requirement for a new interceptor able to engage and destroy the USAF's planned North American B-70 Valkyrie Mach 3 bomber. Mikoyan and Sukhoi both flew experimental research aircraft to explore the problems of flight at such high speeds. The success of Mikoyan's Ye-166 and the disappointing results from Sukhoi's T-37 led to the Mikoyan bureau being given the contract to develop the new Ye-26 fighter.

The use of titanium was reserved for areas of high thermal stress, such as the wing leading edge. Most of the fuselage was made from steel, although conventional aluminium alloys were also used wherever possible. To power the aircraft, the Mikoyan team adopted the Tumanski R-31 turbojet used in the Yastreb drone, installing two in the Ye-26's wide rear fuselage.

Remotely Piloted Vehicles (RPVs) have a short life compared with manned aircraft, so tend to have simple engines, with fewer compressor and turbine stages than longer-lived designs. Tumanski's R-31 follows this philosophy, having a single shaft carrying five compressor stages and driven by a single turbine. At subsonic speeds such a design is fairly inefficient, but at speeds of above Mach 2 the aircraft's air intake adds more compression, allowing the engine to operate more like a ramjet than a conventional tubojet, improving efficiency. Foxbat's special T-6 fuel, which combines a low freezing point with a high flash point, may be another item borrowed from the Yastreb drone.

The Ye-26 first flew in 1964. Production deliveries started in 1968, but service introduction seems to have been delayed until around 1970 as the result of stability and control problems. By 1970, or 1971 at the latest, the new Soviet fighter, now known as the MiG-25, was in service. Examples deployed to Egypt soon

Below: The MiG-25R reconnaissance aircraft exists in two versions – the camera-equipped Foxbat B seen here, and the Foxbat D elint (electronic intelligence-gathering) aircraft.

afterwards were of a reconnaissance model, and flew with impunity over Israeli-occupied Sinai, immune to interception by IDFAF Phantoms or Hawk SAMs. In the early 1970s, Soviet Foxbats were to fly with similar impunity over Iranian territory, a practise which was suddenly halted in 1977 when the Imperial Iranian Air Force's first F-14 Tomcats armed with long-range AGM-54A Phoenix missiles became operational.

Tube Technology's advantage

The Foxbat A interceptor carried the I/J band Fox Fire radar. The fact that this set was based on thermionic tubes rather than semiconductor devices was first quoted as evidence of the backwardness of the Soviet electronics industry. More recently it is given as evidence that the the Soviets were creating tube-based avionics which could not be knocked out by the electro-magnetic pulse (EMP) from high-altitude nuclear explosions. The truth is more prosaic – tube technology was far from obsolete in the late 1950s when the design of Foxbat and its weaponry was begun. Fox Fire was matched with the massive AA-6 Acrid missile, a huge weapon whose warhead was intended to inflict massive damage to high-altitude targets.

The long shadow which Foxbat had cast over Western defense planning was finally lifted in September 1976 when a Soviet pilot, Viktor Belenko, defected to Japan, landing his Foxbat A at Hakodate airport. By the time that the aircraft was handed back to the Soviet Union, it had been stripped down by US and Japanese intelligence officers and examined in the minutest detail. The Soviets later claimed that the aircraft returned them had had many of its systems missing and was virtually a write-off.

Perhaps the biggest surprise which the West

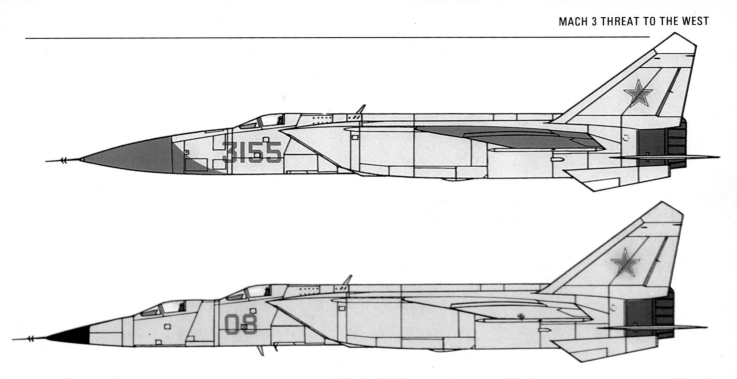

had was the news that the aircraft's top speed was not the Mach 3 observed by E-3 AWACS aircraft, but Mach 2.8. The high-speed targets sighted deep within Warsaw Pact airspace by the E-3s had been Yastreb drones.

Foxbat A had been deployed in only modest numbers, and a hasty program of modification was carried out to blunt the impact of the West's intelligence 'booty' gleaned from Belenko's

aircraft. Soviet Air Force deployment of Foxbat A was kept to around 300, and the aircraft was allowed to stay in production for export to selected client states such as Algeria, Libya and Syria.

At the same time, the Soviets hurriedly created a new interceptor variant, the MiG-25M Foxbat E. Some authorities believe that the aircraft was equipped with the new radar

Top: A Ye-26 prototype with painted nose.

Above: The nose section of the MiG-25U Foxbat C trainer is extended to make space for a second cockpit.

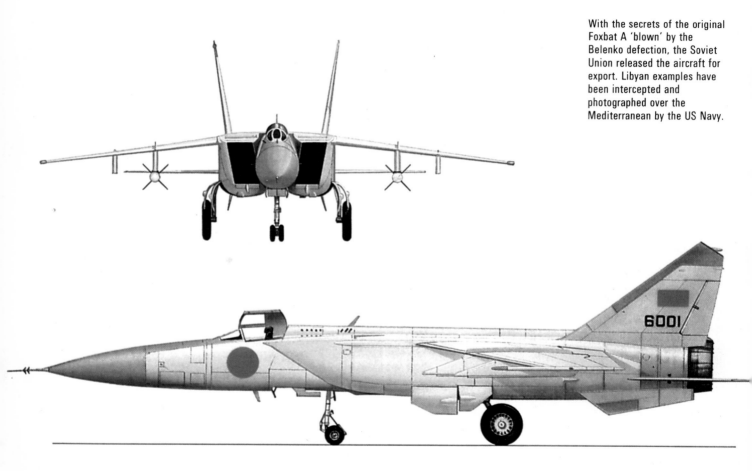

With the secrets of the original Foxbat A 'blown' by the Belenko defection, the Soviet Union released the aircraft for export. Libyan examples have been intercepted and photographed over the Mediterranean by the US Navy.

6001

Mikoyan MiG-25 Foxbat A

Role: single-seat interceptor
Length: 78 ft 1.75 in (23.8 m)
Height: 20 ft 0.25 in (6.10 m)
Wingspan: 45 ft 9 in (13.95 m)
Weights: empty 44,000 lb (20,000 kg);
   max. takeoff 82,500 lb (37,400 kg)
Powerplant(s): two Tumanski R-31 turbojets
Rating: 20,500 lb (9,300 kg) dry thrust, 27,010 lb
   (12,250 kg) with after burners
Tactical radius: 610 nm (1,130 km)
Max. speed: Mach 2.83
Ceiling: 80,000 ft (24,400 m) **Armament:** four
   AA-6 Acrid air-to-air missiles

being developed for the latter MiG-31 Foxhound, but a more likely candidate is one of the radars used in the MiG-23 Flogger. Other changes introduced on Foxbat E are an IR sensor mounted under the nose, and the use of a more powerful Tumanski (probably an uprated version of the R-31).

While Foxbat has never been exported to the Warsaw Pact, more than 600 are in Soviet service. More than 300 Foxbat A interceptors have been modified to the MiG-25M Foxbat E standard. The new Foxbat F is a dedicated defense suppression aircraft armed with AS-11 anti-radiation missiles, and can be recognised by a dielectric panel on the fuselage side just aft of the radome. Around 170 MiG-25R reconnaissance aircraft are also in Soviet service, most being the camera-equipped Foxbat B, a smaller portion of the fleet being the Foxbat D elint aircraft.

Following his 1976 defection, Belenko told US intelligence officials that a much-improved two-seat version of Foxbat was under development. In his 1985 book 'Aviation Fact file: MiGs', Bill Sweetman suggests that the new aircraft was developed following the poor performance of the Soviet-built fighters during the 'Operation Linebacker II' B-52 raids on Hanoi in 1972.

The prototype MiG-31 Foxhound flew for the

Right: The new MiG-31 Foxhound is a two-seat Mach 2.5 interceptor armed with AA-9 Amos missiles.

first time in the mid-1970s, but did not enter service until 1985, three years later than had been assumed in earlier accounts. More than 160 are now in Soviet Air Force service, and production is still under way. Two-thirds of the fleet serves with the Air Defense Force, the remainder with Frontal Aviation.

Foxhound's Metallurgy

One feature likely to be unchanged in the new aircraft is the use of steel rather than aluminium alloy. Foxhound has a top speed of Mach 2.4, for which aluminium alloy would be perfectly adequate. Wherever practical, the Foxhound designers will have switched from steel to

aluminium, but the older material will have been retained in many areas in order to avoid the need to invest in new jigs and production tooling. In other areas, titanium may have been substituted for steel.

Foxbat was never intended for dogfighting, the structure having been designed to pull a maximum of 5g rather than the 9g of most current fighters. The redesigned structure has probably been restressed to accept a higher load factor, although the aircraft remains essentially a straight-line interceptor. Evidence of this strengthening may be seen on the top surface of the wing. Foxhound and Foxbat both have a prominent wing fence, but the newer aircraft does not have the stiffening rib seen outboard of the fence on the MiG-25.

Wings and tail surfaces are all obviously closely modelled on those of Foxbat, with most of the changes being confined to the fuselage. This was stretched in length, and a second cockpit added in the location occupied by an avionics bay on the earlier aircraft. Small leading edge root extensions (LERX) have been added, and the jetpipes are extended.

The LERX will give the aircraft a bit more maneuverability to match its role, but the main purpose may have been a generate extra lift forward of the wing, compensating for the weight of the extended forward fuselage.

Early descriptions of the MiG-31 suggested that it would use the 30,865 lb (14,000 kg) thrust Tumansky R-31F, a derivative of the R-31 en-

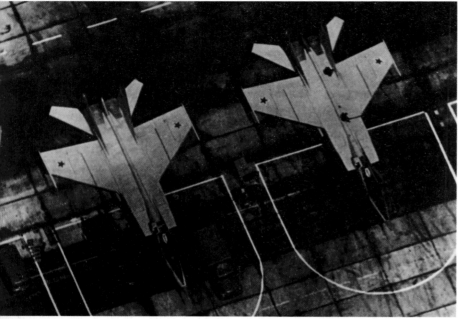

Above: Parked at an unidentified airfield, these MiG-25R Foxbat D elint aircraft seem to have been targetted by a Western recce aircraft.

suming that the new engine is shorter than the R-31, a substantial amount of space will have become available within the fuselage for extra internal fuel.

Another change in this area concerns the vertical stabilizers. On Foxbat, these are mounted high on the curved rear surface of the engine bays. The narrower-diameter afterburner nozzles of Foxhound's engines lie fully within the space between the twin vertical surfaces. In order to keep these surfaces at the correct spacing and height, maintaining the proven MiG-25 aerodynamic layout, they are now mounted on a narrow fairing which rises from the sides of the aft fuselage.

The inlets have been simplified. A fixed air-spillage door similar to that seen on the F-14 occupies the space formerly assigned to a rectangular duct used to bleed air from the Foxbat inlet, and the water/methanol injection pipe has been deleted. On Foxbat, this ran along the outer top edge to a point forward of the lower lip, allowing the mixture to be sprayed into the inlet at high Mach numbers, cooling the air and allowing extra thrust to be generated.

Foxhound is fitted with a new pulse-Doppler radar incorporating full look-down/shoot-down capability, and track-while-scan operating modes. During flight trials in the late 1970s, this radar guided AA-9 missiles against a range of difficult targets. A Foxbat trials aircraft equipped with the Foxhound radar was able to

gine currently flying in the Foxbat, but this seems unlikely. The R-31 was virtually a super-charged ramjet whose operating cycle was optimised for flight at above Mach 2.6. It would be very inefficient at lower speeds, so it is likely that a new turbofan in the 31,000 lb (14,000 kg) thrust class is used. Use of a new engine is conformed by the generally slimmer lines of the rear fuselage. The jetpipes protrude much further than those on Foxbat. As-

conduct near simultaneous attacks against four medium-altitude targets, demonstrate shoot-down attacks from a 20,000 ft (6,100 m) cruising height against targets of 1 sq m radar cross section flying at altitudes of 200 ft (60 m), and launch a 'snap-up' missile attack from 54,000 ft (16,500 m) against a target flying at 70,000 ft (21,000 m).

Tactical radius is 1,135 nm according to the US DoD, a figure well in excess of the 780 nm quoted for Foxbat. Both probably reflect 'best-case' conditions rather than a realistic military mission. Other authorities such as Bill Gunston and Bill Sweetman settle for a more modest 800 – 810 nm and this seems a more dependable figure.

Above: Until the MiG-29 Fulcrum made its international debut at the 1988 Farnborough Air Show, this high-performance Soviet fighter had only been glimpsed during brief interceptions over international waters.

49

Impressive Fulcrum

Below: This drawing of a single-seat MiG-29 Fulcrum A shows the novel configuration of the new fighter, although it is now known that the small fairing under the nose is an ILS antenna and not a sensor as depicted here. The latest Flucrum C version of the aircraft has a revised dorsal which holds extra internal fuel.

One of the important few fighters in Soviet service is the Mikoyan MiG-29 Fulcrum. This agile 'dogfighter' was only deployed in the early 1980s, but more is known about it than is the case with older types – the result of two aircraft having seen sent to the 1988 Farnborough air show.

Normal Soviet engineering practise involves flight testing several designs using alternative wing planforms approved by TsAGI – the Soviet Central Aerodynamics and Hydrodynamics Institute. In the 1950s, the TsAGI-approved tailed delta configuration was applied to both a small Mikoyan fighter and a larger longer-ranged Sukhoi interceptor, so it came as no surprise to the West when

the same philosophy was re-used in the late 1970s to create a new generation of advanced fighters.

The MiG-29 and the Su-27 were designed in the mid-1970s, and flight trials were under way at the Ramenskoye test center near Moscow by 1978. US reconnaissance satellites soon detected the new aircraft as well as the Su-25. At this early stage, the smaller Mikoyan aircraft was assigned the temporary designation RAM-L, while the heavier Sukhoi interceptor became the RAM-K.

First reports claimed that the larger aircraft had variable-geometry wings. If this was the case, the VG prototype was soon joined by a fixed-wing derivative. It is more likely, however, that alternative sweep angles were tested on several prototypes, thus giving the impression that VG was being used. Some reports have suggested that the MiG-29 was also tested with alternative wing planforms.

Following flight trials, a common configuration was selected for both aircraft. This combined a moderately swept wing, F-16/F-18-style long leading-edge root extensions (LERX), twin vertical stabilizers and twin engines. Like the Grumman F-14, Fulcrum has widely separated engine bays, whose inlets offer a simple and direct path for the airflow to the engines. Prototype MiG-29s were probably powered by the Tumansky R-25 used in third-generation MiG-21s, but the production air-

craft are fitted with Tumanski R-33 low bypass ratio turbofans of 18,300 lb (8,300 kg) thrust in afterburner.

The US Navy's F-18 uses the compact General Electric F404 engine, a powerplant whose modest dimensions allow the inlets to be located well aft of the LEX leading edge, benefitting from the latter's effect on the local airflow. On the MiG-29, the inlets are located close to the leading edge of the LERX, so are unable to help guide air into the inlets at high angles of attack.

TsAGI can hardly have been unaware of the advantages of aft-located inlets. The fact that these were not adopted on the MiG-29 suggests that the engines used in both aircraft are much longer than Western engines of similar thrust.

The Smoking MiG

Although the RD-33 is in the same thrust class as the F404, its size is probably closer to that of the J79 turbojet which powers the F-4 Phantom. To judge by the amount of smoke the MiG29 produced when flying at the Farnborough Air Show in 1988, the engine probably runs at a combustor temperature nearer to that of the J79 than that of the latest generation of US engines. Some observers believed that smoke emission occurred when the pilot made sudden changes in throttle setting, but in practise it corresponded to the application of full military power.

Many first-generation Western turbofans proved temperamental, but the RD-33 is made of sterner stuff. When the aircraft is flown through a tail-slide maneuver, the reverse airflow which the engines experience as the aircraft falls back tail-first does not disturb those Tumanskis. One highly unusual feature of the engine installation is the ability of the inlet ramp to swing down to the point where it closes the inlet, leaving the engine to draw its air supply via louvres in the upper surface of the inlet duct. The engine operates in this mode while the aircraft is on the ground, a novel but effective way of preventing the inlets from sucking in foreign objects which might damage the engine. This ingenious touch of Soviet engineering ensures that the MiG-29 can operate out of rough airstrips.

Although the general appearance of the aircraft is smooth and rounded, the cockpit sides are flat plates – a component only clearly seen under the right lighting conditions. This is a feature noted on some earlier MiGs, and probably indicates the presence of armor plating intended to protect the pilot.

First flight of the MiG-29 was in 1977. Devel-

India's first MiG-29s were
imported from the Soviet Union,
and assembled in India by
Soviet technicians. Later
examples will be built under
licence in India, as were the
MiG-21, MiG-23 and MiG-27.

opment was protracted by Soviet standards, with the first aircraft not becoming operational until 1983. First export customers were India and Syria, but the type was not exported to the Soviet Union's Warsaw Pact allies until May 1988.

When the aircraft made its Farnborough debut it attracted much uncritical media attention. Its flying display was good, particularly the much-vaunted tail slide maneuver, and the difficult-to-fly knife-edge pass along the flight line. Less impressive was the roll rate (well below that of the F-16) and a tendency for speed to bleed off during maneuvers.

Many observers were surprised to learn that Fulcrum uses conventional hydraulic controls rather than the more modern fly-by-wire, but this should have been predictable given the Soviet fondness for simplicity. As the McDonnell Douglas Eagle has shown, high agility does not demand the use of fly-by-wire controls.

The MiG-29 is fitted with a modern pulse-Doppler radar which allows 'look-down/shoot-down' attacks against low-level targets. Soviet designation is NO-93, but the set's NATO designation has been variously reported as 'Flash Dance' and 'Slot Back'. Although much more effective than the radars carried by the MiG-21 and -23, it does not match the capability of the US radars in the F-15 and F-18. Maximum range against fighter-sized targets is around 54 nm (100 km).

Right: Late-model Su-17/20/22 aircraft such as these Lyulka-powered Soviet Air Force Fitter H feature a lengthened and deeper forward fuselage, plus a dorsal spine which probably houses avionics and extra fuel.

A glass dome just ahead of the cockpit contains a steerable optical head shared by an infra-red search and track (IRST) sensor and a laser rangefinder. The IRST provides an alternative to radar, and similar units have been fitted to US fighters such as the F-14 Tomcat and some models of F-4 Phantom. What it cannot do is provide range information, and the Soviet decision to install a laser rangefinder is a neat solution to this problem. The laser also gives highly accurate ranging during gun attacks, increasing hit probability.

Flanker

In 1985 a Soviet TV program gave the West its first unclassified glimpse of the Su-27. The aircraft shown was not the current standard, but one of the prototypes. It was thus in no way representative of the service aircraft. In general appearance, the Su-27 is broadly similar to the Grumman F-14, particularly in areas such as the forward fuselage, cockpit, and widely separated engine bays. Flanker is the first Soviet Mach 2 fighter to adopt a high-visibility 'teardrop' cockpit canopy. Previous Soviet designs have had poor rearward visibility, and even the MiG-29 has a canopy much inferior to those of US types such as the F-15, F-16 and F-18.

The first version of the aircraft had a wing with curved tips, the configuration used on the MiG-29. On the production version, the wingtip

Above: Another view of Sukhoi Su-27 Flanker no. 27, the aircraft which created an international incident in 1987 when it collided with the propellors of a P-3 Orion of 333 Sqn, Royal Norwegian Air Force. Both aircraft suffered only minor damage, and were able to return to their respective bases.

is clipped, terminating in a missile launch rail. Two prominent wing fences present on the prototypes have been deleted.

On the prototypes, the vertical tail surfaces were located high on the fuselage sides and well forward of the aft end of the fuselage, spanning the gap between the wing trailing edge and the front edge of the horizontal tailplane. This location was pioneered by Northrop on the YF-17 and adopted for the F-18 Hornet, but on the US aircraft these surfaces are canted outwards to bring them into the path of the lift-inducing vortexes streaming backwards from the LERXes. This outward tilt is not needed on the Su-27. Thanks to the widely separated engine bays, the aft fuselage is much wider than on Hornet, bringing the tail fins aft of LERXes. They could thus be mounted vertically, but had to be more than 12 ft (3.6 m) high to ensure directional stability at high angles of incidence.

On production aircraft, the vertical fins and horizontal stabilizers are mounted not on the fuselage, but on F-15-style fuselage beams outboard of the engines. Flight trials may have indicated the need to increase the distance between the vertical fins, or a change of powerplant may have dictated the removal of the fin-support structure from the revised engine bay.

Like the F-14 and the MiG-29, the Su-27 has widely separated engine bays. Like the Mikoyan design, its inlets are positioned close to the LERX leading edge. The engine bays are about 35 ft (10.5 m) long, only slightly longer than those on the F-14 and F-15. This suggests that the aircraft uses a powerplant in the same performance class as the Pratt & Whitney F100 or the General Electric F110. When analyzing the aircraft for a US magazine in 1987, I estimated that the inlet size suggested the use of engines in the 25,000 lb (11,000 kg) thrust class. Prototypes may have been powered by a pair of Tumanski R-29 turbojets, but the service aircraft engine uses a custom-designed engine. The Tumanski R-32 is thought to be a new turbofan developing 29,995 lb (13,600 kg) of afterburning thrust.

Early US assessments of the Flanker radar published in the late 1970s predicted that its pulse-Doppler radar would have a search range of up to 130 nm and the ability to track targets at 100 nm. These figures do not seem unrealistic. Flanker's nose radome has a diameter of more than 4 ft (1.2 m), so is able to house an antenna larger than the 36 in (91 cm) diameter unit on the West's largest fighter radar – the Hughes AWG-9 carried by the F-14.

Like the MiG-29, Flanker has a glass dome mounted just forward of the cockpit canopy. This presumably houses a combined FLIR and laser rangefinder system similar to that on the Mikoyan aircraft. To judge by the aircraft involved in the Norwegian P-3 incident, a second EO system is fitted inside the canopy. Mounted to the port side of the aircraft's HUD, this is probably a stabilized optical sight offering some degree of magnification.

Flanker's Chances Against the Eagle

Top speeds of Mach 2.2 or 2.3 at altitude have been suggested, and the aircraft will certainly be supersonic (around Mach 1.1–1.2) at sea level. The US DoD estimates the tactical radius of Flanker to be 810 nm (1,500 km) for a subsonic intercept missile with external fuel tanks. This figure has been widely accepted, but an alternative figure of 650 to 700 nm (1,200–1,300 km) suggested in 1986 by Bill Sweetman probably reflects more realistic operating conditions. If my weight figures are broadly correct, and published estimates of the Su-27's wing area are not too wide of the mark, Flanker will almost certainly be able to match the air-combat maneuverability of the F-15 Eagle.

The Su-27 can carry up to eight AAMs, early reports suggesting that these would be the 25 nm range radar-guided AA-9 missile carried by the MiG-31 Foxhound, but the aircraft is now known to carry a mix of types. These include the medium-range AA-10 Alamo, and the short range AA-8 Aphid or AA-11 Archer. These are supplemented by a single six-barrelled rotary cannon carried in the starboard side of the center fuselage.

Some observers credit Flanker with a secondary air-to-ground strike capability, and suggest that up to 13,000 lb (6,000 kg) of ordnance may be carried. If so, then strike would be a secondary role. The aircraft is primarily an interceptor, and its large wing area would make it sensitive to turbulence at low level.

In the past, the heavy interceptors used by the Soviet Union for home defense were aircraft designed to make powerful attacks on bomber targets. Little attention was paid to the prospect of fighter-versus-fighter combat. All this has changed with the arrival of the Su-27. The presence of LERXes confirms that the aircraft is a highly agile type able to engage NATO fighters. Like the USAF, the Soviet Air Force seems to be planning an F-15/F-16 style 'hi-lo mix', and likely roles for the Su-27 could include engaging NATO fighters in long-range missile-versus-missile duels before closing for

Libyan MiG-23 Flogger E armed with AA-2 Atoll missiles. The small Jay Bird radar and low-performance Atoll missiles give the aircraft little air-to-air combat capability in other than good weather.

medium and short-range combat, or acting as escorts for strike formations.

This aircraft entered service early in 1986, but the delivery rate was slow. Late that year the US DoD estimated that only 15 aircraft were in service, a figure which had risen to only 50 a year later. By the end of 1988, total deliveries to the Air Defense Force was little more than 100. The Soviet electronics industry seems to have serious problems in turning out Flanker's com-plex avionics. Late in 1985, 'Interavia AirLetter' claimed that 'hundreds' of aircraft were parked at the Komsomolsk plant awaiting radar equipment.

It seems likely that complexity and high cost may rule out Flanker being deployed on any-thing like the scale of the MiG-23. A fleet of no more than 300 by the end of 1990 seems real-istic, and it may be the mid-1990s before the total passes the 1,000 mark.

Opposite: The original (short) pattern of nose radome and the small EW antennas mounted high on the sides of the air inlet identify this Su-24 strike aircraft as the Fencer C version.

The Quality Gap Narrows

Having gained useful experience in applying VG to a tactical strike aircraft, the Sukhoi team turned its hand in the late 1960s to the problem of creating a modern replacement for the Yak-28 Brewer. The new design differed in one important respect from the Western designs. Since the aircraft was intended for tactical missions rather than the long-range operations envisaged for the F-111, less emphasis was placed on subsonic range. Thrust to weight ratio of a lightly loaded F-111A was only 0.45 at take-off, while the Sukhoi team had its sights set on values well above 0.6.

The Su-24, Fencer, has often been regarded as a 'mini-F-111', but early descriptions have tended to underestimate its size and weight. The aircraft which took shape in the prototype shop was much slimmer than its GD rival, but only a few feet (around a metre) shorter. Empty weight was probably around 42,000 lb (19,000 kg) rising a 64,000 lb (29,000 kg) clean take-off weight.

Fencer required an engine in the ten-tonne-thrust class, preferably a turbofan. Soviet engine designers were slow to adopt the turbofan, so in the late 1960s the only candidate was a turbojet. Lyulka's AL-21F was already well-known to the design team, being the latest model of an engine widely used in Sukhoi types such as the Su-7, -9, -11 and -17. It was used for the prototypes, and for the initial Fencer A production version.

Like the MiG-23, Su-24 is not thought to have continuously variable sweep, but to offer the pilot a choice of several fixed settings. These are selected manually, and are thought to be 16, 45, 55 and 68 degrees. Eight pylons are provided for stores, one swivelling pylon under each outer wing, one fixed pylon under each fixed glove section, and four under the fuselage. Like the MiG-23, Fencer uses differential spoilers for roll control, but the trailing-edge flaps are double-slotted rather than the single-slotted configuration used on the Mikoyan aircraft.

Date of first flight is not known, but probably took place in 1969 or 1970. Development was fairly protracted, with the first units not becoming operational until December 1974. The new aircraft was kept under wraps for five years, deployed only at bases within the Soviet Union. In 1979 a single regiment was briefly deployed to Templin air base in East Germany, allowing snooping cameras to obtain a first clear glimpse of the initial production model.

Fencer A seems to have been a relatively austere interim version intended to allow Frontal Aviation to build up experience in operating their first modern long-range fighter-bomber. For the first time, FA crews

Right: Su-24 Fencer C at low level with wing slats extended. The broad rear fuselage offers ample room for two massive engines each in the ten-ton thrust class.

These early drawings of an Su-24 were prepared at at a time when the West had only seen the aircraft during one brief deployment to Templin in East Germany. They show the original Fencer A version, a model rapidly supplanted by the better-equipped B and C variants.

Sukhoi Su-24 Fencer B

Role: strike aircraft
Length: 69 ft 10 in (21.29 m)
Height: 18 ft (5.5 m)
Wingspan: 34 ft 5 in to 55 ft 5 in (10.5–17.5 m)
Weights: empty 42,000 lb (19,000 kg); loaded 64,000 lb (29,000 kg); max. takeoff 87,000 lb (39,500 kg)
Powerplant(s): two Tumanski R-29B turbojet
Rating: see under MiG-23
Tactical radius: 970 nm (1,800 km) with two tons of ordnance plus external fuel
Max. speed: Mach 2.1 at altitude
Ceiling: 54,000 ft (16,500 m)
Armament: up to 24,000 lb (11,00 kg) of ordnance, plus one 30 mm cannon

An Indian Air Force MiG-29 Flucrum patrols near the Himalayas. Soon after its Soviet Air Force debut, the type was rapidly cleared for export to nations such as India, North Korea, Syria, Iraq, and Jugoslavia. East Germany was the first Warsaw Pact export customer.

had a mount capable of attacking targets over most of Western Europe, delivering the ordnance within 180 ft (55 m) of the target in all weathers. The two-man crew sit side-by-side on zero-zero ejector seats within an F-111-style cockpit. A weapons system operator handles an avionics suite which introduced Frontal Aviation crews to a new level of complexity, including terrain-following and navigation/attack radars, digital computers and HUD. A small fairing directly under the nose probably contained a laser rangefinder.

Fencer's Impressive Armory

Ordnance carried on the aircraft's pylons includes free-falling iron or 'smart' bombs, fuel-air explosives, or specialized anti-tank or anti-runway weapons. Missiles known to be carried by Fencer include the AS-7 Kerry command-guided missile, the AS-9 Kyle anti-radar weapon, As-10 Karen laser-guided or AS-11 TV-guided missile, AS-12 Kegler, AS-13 and AS-14 Kedge. Early reports claiming that AA-2 Atoll or AA-8 Aphid missiles can be carried have never been substantiated.

Two prominent bulged fairings are located beneath the fuselage and forward of the main undercarriage. The starboard fairing contains a 30 mm rotary cannon, while the smaller unit on the port side probably contains an ammunition magazine. Two small dorsally-mounted airbrakes partially cover these fairings, conforming to their shape, and perhaps forming part of the fairing skin.

While the new aircraft entered service in growing numbers, the design team was at work on new variants intended to fully meet FA requirements. First move was to get rid of the veteran AL-7F engine, a design which dated back to the 1950s. The rear fuselage and engine bays were modified to accept the more fuel-efficient Tumanski R-29B developed for the MiG-23. This was a relatively straightforward task. A cooling air intake was added at the base of the fin, and the parachute brake fairing was increased in size.

The fact that Fencer is often seen with a large 600-gal (3,000 l) tank under each glove raises speculation that the designers may have got the balance wrong in packing in the engine power at the expense of internal fuel, leaving the aircraft short of range. The recontouring of the rear fuselage introduced by the Fencer B could be the result of a drag-reduction program.

Major avionics improvements had to await the Fencer C version fielded in the early 1980s. New antenna fairings located on the sides of the intakes (level with and just ahead of the gloves) and near the top of the fin tip indicate the presence of what could be a better ESM system able to replace the widely used Sirena 3, although a small bullet fairing at the rear edge of the rudder (a feature widely associated with Sirena) is still present just aft of the new fintop

antenna. The flight-control system was also improved, with a new pitot head being added to the aircraft nose, and a twin-probe sensor under the forward fuselage just forward of the nosewheel doors.

Fencer D was a more extensive redesign. The nose was stretched by 30 in (75 cm), presumably to provide larger avionics bays. The fin was increased in area, and now has a distinct kink in its leading edge. This does not seem to have been the only aerodynamic fix needed; the pylon under the glove has been increased in size, and has been extended over the upper side of the glove, forming a distinct fence. The chin-mounted sensors have been deleted, as have the probes added on the C model. A new curved-profile fairing mounted just aft of the nosewheel bay is thought to house

Above: For an aircraft first fielded in the early 1980s, Fencer C has remarkably smokey engines.

a steerable electro-optical system, perhaps a laser designator.

Still under development as this text was prepared in the winter of 1988, Fencer E is thought to be an EW aircraft designed to replace the Yak-28 Brewer E. Little is known about this version, and details of a reported Fencer F are even sketchier. The latter could be a dedicated reconnaissance model reported in 1987 to be under development for Naval Aviation. This was expected to carry an internal sensor suite, and to have a secondary role of launching anti-ship missiles.

Soviets Miss a Trick

It is always easy to be wise in retrospect, but I can't help thinking that the Soviet failure to build an equivalent to the McDonnell Douglas F-4 Phantom was for the Warsaw Pact probably the biggest missed opportunity of the 1960s aerospace scene. In 1962, four years after the F-4 first flew, the Soviet Air Force issued its own specification for a twin-engined Mach 2 interceptor. They could have asked for an aircraft in the Phantom performance class. A suitable engine already existed in the form of the Tumanski R-11 turbojet (an engine already earmarked for further development into more powerful versions), and given a fast-paced program a hot new fighter could have been created and fielded in 1969–1971 to match the F-4s flying over the skies of Vietnam and Sinai.

What the 1962 specification demanded, and what the Sukhoi team actually built, was a very different sort of warplane – a classic climb, dash, intercept and return fighter of the sort traditionally favored by the PVO Strany for defense of Soviet airspace. For its new interceptor, the PVO Strany effectively asked for a scaled-up version of its existing Su-9/11.

The new design abandoned one feature of the Su-9 and Su-11, the nose inlet and center body-mounted radar. Side intakes had been tested on the experimental mid-1950s T-49, T-5 and P-1 designs, giving the experience needed to design the new interceptor's intakes.

First flight of the resulting Su-15 Flagon took place in 1965, and ten were available by the following July to take part in the huge Domodedovo Air Show alongside an experimental STOL Su-15VD version. NATO reporting names for these aircraft were Flagon A and B. Deployment of the Su-15 should have been swift, given that the aircraft's Uragan 5B Skip Spin radar was reported to be a derivative of that carried by the Su-11, and that its AA-3 Anab missiles were the same as those on the Su-11. It seems likely that the aircraft's radar had little in common with the smaller set in the Su-11, and that avionics development accounted for the delays in fielding the Su-15. First true deployment was not until 1971, although pre-series aircraft may have equipped trials units before then.

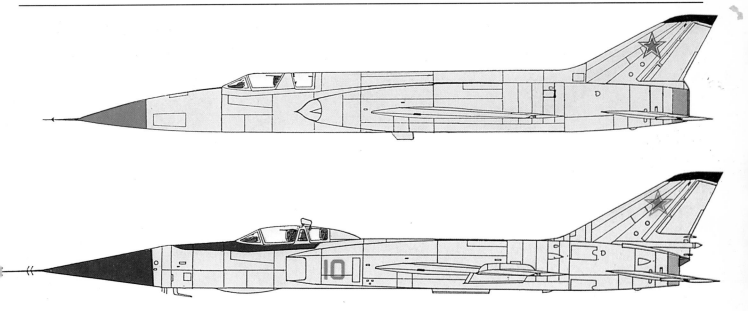

A two-seat Flagon C trainer was also deployed, but longer term plans were based on a much improved version thought to be designated Su-21, and known to NATO as Flagon E. This was powered by the uprated R-13 engine, and featured larger intakes, twin nose wheels, a revised wing and improved radar. The new wing is of compound sweep, the inboard section have a leading edge swept at around 53

degrees, the outboard being swept at around 37 degrees. At the point around midspan where the sweep changes, there is a narrow unswept section and a large wing fence. NATO reporting name for the new radar in 'Twin Scan', and some sources have speculated a possible relationship with the 'Fox Fire' set carried by the MiG-25. A later Flagon F version has a radome of ogival shape rather than the

Top: First flown in 1957, the Sukhoi P-1 two-seat interceptor tested side inlets.

Above: The Su-15U Flagon C two-seat trainer is based on the original Su-15 Flagon a fighter.

69

Flagon F was the final production model of the Su-15 series. It is thought to be designated Su-21, a designation shared with the earlier Flagon E. The latter introduced the break in the continuity of the wing leading edge, and had a conical radome similar to that on the Flagon A.

Sukhoi Su-21 Flagon F

Role: all-weather interceptor
Length: 68 ft 0 in (20.5 m)
Wingspan: 34 ft 6 in (10.53 m)
Weights: empty 25,000 lb (11,500 kg); loaded 37,000 lb (17,000 kg); max takeoff 42,000 lb (19,000 kg)
Powerplant(s): two Tumanski R-13F2-300 turbojets
Rating: 15,875 lb (7,200 kg) with afterburner
Tactical radius: 390 nm (725 km)
Max. speed: Mach 2.1
Armament: Two AA-8 Aphid and two AA-3 Anab missiles

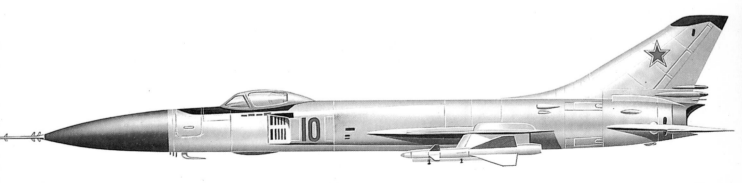

The general lines of the two-seat MiG-31 Foxhound clearly mark the aircraft as a development of the older MiG-25 Foxbat. A puzzling feature of the aircraft shown here is the different nozzles on the port and starboard engines!

original conical pattern, and all Soviet Air Force Flagon E aircraft have been updated to this standard.

The Su-15 and Su-21 were never exported, although a squadron of Su-15s was briefly deployed to Egypt in 1971. The Su-15 has been retired, but the Su-21 still plays a major role with the Soviet Air Force. The 550 or so still in service are split between Frontal Aviation (300+) and the Air Defense Force (200+).

Bomber-sized Fighter

Anyone catching a glimpse of the massive Tu-28P Fiddler interceptor might be forgiven for assuming that this large swept-wing aircraft was a bomber. The error would be understandable, given that the aircraft owes its origins to a mid-1950s Tupolev bomber design, the Tu-98 Backfin. Developed at the same time as the rival Ilyushin-54 Blowlamp, the Tu-98 was an attempt to design a medium bomber capable of marginally supersonic flight. Wherever possible, the Tupolev team tried to use technology from the subsonic Tu-16 bomber, but packed the engines side by side within the rear fuselage, rather than in the wing roots. The Tu-16 had used the RD-3M turbojet, but the greater speed of the Tu-98 dictated the use of two of Lyulka's afterburning AL-7 engines. To feed these with air, the ducts ran forward over the wing to inlets located on the upper sides of the fuselage just aft of the cockpit.

Flight tested in 1956, it was rejected (as was the Il-54) as offering little advantage over the Tu-16. When the Soviet Air Force released a requirement for what was probably a heavy fighter/reconnaissance aircraft, the Tu-98 was the ideal starting point. The rear fuselage was revised, receiving a smaller vertical fin and two ventral strakes, and the main undercarriage was now stowed in fairings at the trailing edge of the wing. A new forward fuselage housed the two man-crew seated in tandem, a large nose radome for the aircraft's search radar, and a ventral mapping/air surveillance radar.

This aircraft, designated Tu-102 was publicly displayed in 1961. It was armed with two AA-5 Ash missiles, one under each wing. Custom-designed for the new fighter, these were more than 17 ft (5 m) long, 12 in (30 cm) in dia, and weighed around 860 lb (390 kg). Two versions were devised, one with IR guidance and the other with semi-active radar. The new fighter was not fielded in this form, but reworked as a heavy interceptor to meet a 1962 requirement. In its final Tu-128 form, the aircraft was fitted with a huge I-band radar (codenamed 'Big Nose' by NATO), but lost its ventral radar and strakes. It could now carry two Ash missiles under each wing.

First production examples flew for the first time in the mid-1960s, and the type was deployed as the Tu-28P. The aircraft's endurance of around six hours allows it to fly long patrols. It may operate in conjunction with the Tu-126

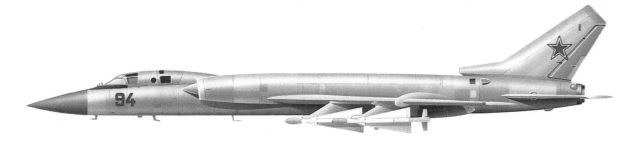

Above: Although two decades old, the massive Tu-28P Fiddler and its custom-designed AA-5 Ash missiles remain in operational service. Designed to deal with the huge Boeing B-52, these elderly interceptors are now faced with the faster and more radar-elusive Rockwell B-1B.

Moss AEW aircraft. No more than 200 were built. Some 90 still serve with the Air Defense Force and a further 25 with Frontal Aviation. Its avionics may have had at least a limited upgrade to maintain their effectiveness, but reports that the aircraft is being replaced by an interceptor version of the Tu-22 Blinder medium bomber remain mere rumour.

When US spy satellites first caught sight of the MiG-29 and Su-27 at Ramenskoye in 1977, they also detected an aircraft of a very different sort, which US intelligence analysts dubbed 'RAM-J'. This was seen as a Soviet equivalent to the USAF's then-new A-10 attack aircraft, a subsonic and heavily armored tankbuster for the close support of ground forces. Indeed, the first artist's impressions of the new aircraft to appear in print showed an A-10 look-alike complete with pod-mounted engines.

The Soviet Union had deployed a heavily armored attack aircraft during World War II. This was the piston-engined Ilyushin Il-2 Shtur-movik. Built in large numbers, it played a prominent part in the Soviet advance from Moscow to Berlin. The follow-on Il-10 offered only marginal improvements, but remained in production until 1949. Two further designs were tested in the late 1940s and early 1950s respectively. These were the piston-engined Il-20 (an incredibly ugly aircraft in the general performance class of the Douglas A-1 Sky-raider) and the jet-powered swept-wing Il-40. The Soviet Air Force rejected both, deciding that the days of the Shturmovik-type armored aircraft were over.

It is not clear why the concept was reborn in the mid-1970s. Some suggest that it was a result of the US A-X program which resulted in the Fairchild A-10, but this seems unlikely. With the exception of a few instances, slavish copying of Western concepts has never been a hallmark of Soviet Air Force or aircraft industry thinking.

In the author's opinion, the aircraft was the

result of a growing emphasis on off-base operations. What Frontal Aviation would ideally have liked would no doubt have been a Soviet equivalent of Harrier, so the Su-25 Frogfoot was probably started in the early 1970s at around the same time as the Yakovlev Yak-38 V/STOL fighter. The latter was always intended for naval use, but the Air Force may originally have seen it as an alternative to the conventional Su-25.

In drawing up the new design, the Sukhoi team took a far more realistic view of the close-support mission than had the USAF. One reason for the rejection of Ilyushin's Il-40 jet-powered Shturmovik in 1953 had been the need for aircraft of this type to be escorted by higher-performance fighters able to keep the other side's fighters at bay. In this respect,

nothing had changed. The Su-25 would have to operate in skies kept largely clear of enemy fighters. The alternative would have been to build an aircraft in the class of the MiG-27.

What the team was determined to do was reduce vulnerability to anti-aircraft guns and to light shoulder-fired SAMs. The US designers of the A-10, and its unsuccessful rival the Northrop A-9, saw nothing wrong with the idea of a close-support aircraft the size of a War II B-25, but their Soviet counterparts had in mind something closer to the size of a normal fighter, and with enough speed to be a difficult target for man-portable SAMs.

The design they created (reported to have the bureau designation 'T-58') has a wingspan of around 50 ft (15 m) and an all-up weight of around 35,000 lb (16,000 kg). Having created

Below: By the standards of the late 1980s, the Su-25 Frogfoot can only be described as 'cheap and cheerful'. Rugged and easy to fly, it proved an effective strike aircraft in Afghanistan. But like US aircraft committed to the Vietnam War two decades earlier, it was unable to break the will of determined guerrilla opponents.

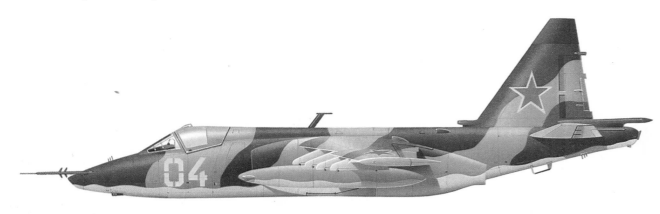

Above: This view of a climbing MiG-25M Foxbat E shows the aircraft's AA-6 Acrid missile armament, and the undernose sensor pod. This model may prove the final Foxbat interceptor – the follow-on Foxbat F is an anti-radar aircraft.

an aircraft about two-thirds the weight of its US counterpart, they installed about 25 per cent more thrust by fitting a pair of non-afterburning Tumanski R-11-300 turbojets, an engine widely used in afterburning form in the MiG-21. It was an wise choice, for while the Lotarev bureau could offer a modern turbofan in the same thrust class, this was a relatively new civil engine while spares and mainten-ance skills for the well-proven R-11 were al-ready available in Frontal Aviation units.

This level of thrust, plus a swept leading edge on the wing and tailplane, resulted in an aircraft capable of a brisk 475 kts (880 km/hr) at low level or Mach 0.7 at altitude. On a strike mission, the Su-25 assigned the NATO report-ing name Frogfoot, has a speed advantage over the A-10 of close to 30 per cent – around 107 kts (198 km/hr). Maximum payload is around 8,800 lb (4,000 kg), about half that of a fully fuelled A-10. Take-off and landing runs are in the A-10 class. With the weapon load kept low, the Su-25 can probably operate happily out of a 1,200 ft (370 m) strip. Combat radius is around 300 nm (560 km).

Like the A-10, The Su-25 incorporates armor. This could be steel rather than the lighter titanium used on the US aircraft, thus account-ing for the Soviet aircraft's unusually high empty weight. Although the sides of the fuse-lage lack the MiG-27-style externally visible slabs of armor claimed in some early descrip-tions, much effort has been put into protecting the pilot. As a result of this armoring, the cockpit allows no rearward visibility other than via mirrors mounted on the sideways-opening canopy. The pilot does have a HUD which probably accepts data from a marked-target indicator located along with a laser ranger behind an optical port in the lower nose. A tiny port on the upper side of the nose is thought to be for a gun camera. A small fairing projecting from the tip of the tail houses a radar-warning receiver antenna, while a flare dispenser is packed into the aircraft's tailcone.

Like the A-10, the Su-25 has a powerful internal gun. This is mounted under the cockpit floor and slightly to the port side of the aircraft centreline. Different sources have described this weapon as a 30 mm M61-style rotary cannon, a twin-barrelled 30 mm cannon, or even as a 23 mm twin-barrelled GSh-23. Eight underwing hard points are provided for general ordnance, while two more close to the wingtips can carry heat-seeking air-to-air missiles for self-defence. The hardpoint closest to the fuselage is plumbed to accept an external fuel tank. Fairings at the wingtips incorporate upward and downward-opening airbrakes.

The Su-25 was first deployed in 1983. The delay in fielding such a simple warplane seems unusual, but no convincing explanation has emerged. Perhaps it experienced aerodynamic problems – the prototypes are reported to have had wing fences not present on the production aircraft, while the latter does have a small dogtooth at around mid-span. The aircraft was soon committed to the war in Afghanistan, where it played a major role in anti-guerilla operations.

By late 1988 more than 250 were in service with Frontal Aviation, and it is significant that most have been deployed in the south-western military districts and in Afghanistan. A single squadron was deployed to the Far East in the summer of 1986. The first to move to the Far East, it is based near Spassk, about 100 miles (160 km) north of Vladivostok. Czechoslovakia and Hungary have each taken delivery of more than 50, starting in 1984, and a growing number have been sold to Iraq.

Assuming that Soviet industry has been able to create effective avionics and missiles to match the aerodynamic performance of its latest fighters, the quality gap between NATO and Warsaw Pact types will become uncomfortably narrow as the number of MiG-29s and Su-27s in service builds up. The US hopes that the Multi-Stage Improvement Plans being applied to its present F-15 Eagle and F-16 Fighting Falcons will restore the qualitative edge which NATO has traditionally enjoyed over the Warsaw Pact, while longer-term plans are focused on the 'stealthy' YF-22A and YF-23A Advanced Tactical Fighters. The latter will not be in large-scale service until the late 1990s, as will Western Europe's new Eurofighter and Rafale. Until then, NATO's air forces must rely on existing types to match the capability of the Soviet designs described in this book.

Above: This MiG-31 Foxhound is almost certainly the same aircraft shown on page 72. The port jet pipe had closed slightly when this photograph was taken, and is smaller in exit area than the fixed unit on the other side.

Simplicity No Longer the Answer

Despite the performance boost its air arms are obtaining from the MiG-29 and Su-27, the Russians still face problems. Soviet aircraft designers are finally closing the gap in fighter performance under which its air arms have labored since the heyday of the MiG-15, but have changed the shape of their industry in doing so. Classic Soviet fighters such as the MiG-21 were designed with mass production in mind. Some of the early MiG-21s displayed a standard of workmanship well below that considered acceptable in the West, but despite this they worked and worked well.

Those days of simplicity are over. With their new-generation warplanes, the Soviet Air Force and its Warsaw Pact allies now face something of the high manufacturing costs and maintenance overheads which have plagued Western defense budgets since the early 1970s. For them – as for the West – the days of the low-cost warplane have ended.

General notes on Specifications

Loaded weights represent the fully fuelled aircraft either without stores, or with a typical light stores loading.

Tactical radius is for a typical combat operaton. If a range of values is given, this indicates the effect of different stores loadings.

Range – where known – is normal ferry range with the maximum payload of external fuel.

Maximum speed is normally at altitude, unless otherwise stated, and is for a clean aircraft.

Ordnance loads quoted under 'Armament' represent maximum values, and will rarely be used in service. Reducing the amount of ordnance carried reduces drag, and thus increases speed and range. Hardpoints may also be needed for jaming pods, or external fuel, limiting the number of weapons which may be carried.

Mikoyan MiG-27 Flogger D

Role: single-seat strike fighter
Length: 52 ft 6 in (16.05 m)
Wingspan: 26 ft 9 in to 46 ft 9 in (8.17–14.25 m)
Weights: empty 24,000 lb (11,000 kg); loaded 34,000 lb (15,500 kg)
Powerplant(s): one Tumanski R-29-300 turbojet
Max. range: 1,350 nm (2,500 km)
Max. speed: Mach 1.7
Armament: one 23 mm rotary cannon plus up to 10,000 lb (4,500 kg) of ordnance

Mikoyan MiG-29 Fulcrum A

Role: fighter
Length: 56 ft 10 in (17.32 m)
Height: 15 ft 3 in (4.73 m)
Wingspan: 37 ft 3 in (11.36 m)
Weights: loaded c. 33,000 lb (15,000 kg)
Powerplant(s): two Tumanski RD-33 low bypass ratio turbofans
Max. range: c. 1,130 nm (2,100 km) with external fuel
Max. speed: greater than Mach 2.3
Armament: AA-10 Alamo and AA-11 Archer missiles, plus one 30 mm cannon

Mikoyan MiG-31 Foxhound

Role: two-seat interceptor
Length: 70 ft 6.5 in (21.5 m)
Wingspan: 45 ft 11 in (14.0 m)
Weights: empty 48,000 lb (21,800 kg); loaded 85,000 lb (38,500 kg)
Powerplant(s): two Tumanski turbofans
Max. speed: Mach 2.4
Armament: four AA-9 air-to-air missiles

Sukhoi Su-20 Fitter C

Role: ground-attack fighter
Length: 61 ft 6 in (18.75 m)
Height: 15 ft 7 in (4.75 m)
Wingspan: 34 ft 9 in to 45 ft 11 in (10.6–14 m)
Weights: empty 22,000 lb (10,000 kg); loaded 31,000 lb (14,000 kg)

Powerplant(s): one Lyulka Al-21F-3 turbojet
Max. speed: Mach 2.1
Armament: two 30 mm NR-30 cannon, plus up to
7,000 lb (3,200 kg) of ordnance

Sukhoi Su-25 Frogfoot

Role: close-support aircraft
Length: 47 ft 6 in (14.5 m)
Wingspan: 50 ft 10 in (15.5 m)
Weights: empty 21,000 lb (9,000 kg); loaded
35,000 lb (16,000 kg)
Powerplant(s): two Tumanski R-13-300 turbojets
Max. speed: Mach 0.7
Armament: One cannon plus up to 9,900 lb
(4,500 kg) of ordnance

Sukhoi Su-7 Flanker

Role: air superiority fighter
Length: 70 ft 10 in (21.6 m)
Wingspan: 48 ft 3 in (14.7 m)
Weights: empty 37,000 lb (16,800 kg); loaded
55,000 lb (25,000 kg)
Powerplant(s): two Tumanski R-32 turbofans
Tactical radius: 810 nm (1,500 km)
Max speed: Mach 2.0 +
Armament: AA-8 Aphid, AA-10 Alamo, and AA-11
Archer missiles, plus one cannon

Tupolev Tu-28P

Role: heavy interceptor
Length: 89 ft 3 in (27.2 m)
Wingspan: 59 ft 4 in (18.1 m)
Weights: empty 54,000 lb (25,000 kg); loaded
88,000 lb (40,000 kg)
Powerplant(s): two Lyulka AL-21F
Max. range: 2,700 nm (5,000 km)
Max. speed: Mach 1.65
Armament: four AA-5 Ash air-to-air missiles

Acknowledgements

The publishers are grateful to the following
organizations for photographs and artworks
appearing in this book: Octopus Books Ltd
(pages 16, 26, 27, 43, 44, 45, 62, 69, 70, 71);
Pilot Press (pages 7, 8, 10, 13, 14, 15, 17, 18,
20, 22, 23, 24, 25, 28, 29, 30, 32, 33, 35, 36, 37,
38, 39, 41, 42, 46, 48, 49, 50, 52, 55, 56, 58, 59,
61, 64, 67, 72, 74, 75, 76, 78) and Quadrant
Picture Library (cover, 2).